SAILING
A Beginner's Manual

John Driscoll

Fernhurst Books
www.fernhurstbooks.co.uk

CONTENTS

Acknowledgements

The author gratefully acknowledges the inspiration of the original RYA National Sailing Coach, Bob Bond, who devised some of the terms and sequences now used throughout the National Training Scheme.
    The publishers would like to thank Tom Gregory and the Emsworth Sailing School for their assistance with the photo sessions, and Mary Allen and Dominic Whelan for sailing the boats. The publishers are indebted to the RYA for permission to use material from their booklet G3.
    The cover photograph is by Roger Lean-Vercoe and the cover design by Behram Kapadia.

**First published in 1987 by Fernhurst Books,
Duke's Path, High Street, Arundel, West Sussex, BN18 9AJ, England.**

ISBN 0 906754 28 3

Design by John Grain
Composition by A & G Phototypesetting, Knaphill
Printed in China through World Print

Welcome to the sport of sailing. It's one of the most popular of all participant sports and you don't have to look far to see why.

Some people are introduced to sailing at a tender age; others take it up as a retirement activity. If you have a competitive spirit, opportunities range from friendly club racing to the Olympics. If you prefer to relax, sailing provides a means to explore the environment and enjoy the challenge of harnessing the elements.

The best way to learn the basic techniques quickly is in a dinghy, which has more sensitivity than a cruising yacht. There are hundreds of recognised sailing schools and centres where qualified instructors will teach you the skills.

This book aims to provide a concise guide to those basic skills, and makes no attempt to teach more than the beginner requires. Once these skills are mastered, the Fernhurst 'Sail to Win' series will help you to improve your boat handling and background knowledge.

John Driscoll
Formerly National Sailing Coach

Water sports are great fun, but there are risks. Safety on the water is a combination of the right equipment and high morale – and one affects the other. If you are warm, and have confidence in your gear, you will be much safer and happier than someone who is cold and nervous.

What to wear

The right clothing will have an enormous effect on your sailing. Too little protection from wind and spray will quickly dampen your enthusiasm, while too many unnecessary layers will slow your movements and make you feel clumsy. Even at the height of summer, the wind and spray will soon cool you down afloat, but the right combination of jeans and sweater, topped off by a lightweight one-piece waterproof suit, will keep you comfortable.

Soft-soled footwear is essential and shoes are preferable to boots which will invariably be shallower than the water you are launching into. Boots can also fill with water when you capsize and make it difficult for you to climb out of the water. If the prospect of sailing around in soggy socks and plimsolls doesn't appeal to you, a pair of neoprene wet-socks is guaranteed to keep your feet warm. That's the first step towards a full neoprene wetsuit, which you'll need if you are going to get involved in dinghy racing or winter sailing.

The other end of the body mustn't be neglected. About a third of body heat loss is through the head, so wear a warm hat or balaclava.

On a warm sunny day ashore all this advice may seem totally out of place but it won't take much cold salt water spray to remind you that it is advice born of experience.

PERSONAL BUOYANCY

A *Buoyancy Aid* looks like a padded waistcoat and the best ones are marked with a British Marine Industries Federation Standard Sign or that of the American National Standards Institute. These are ideal for use in sheltered or inshore waters, providing a measurable degree of buoyancy in a garment which is light in weight, allows freedom of movement and indeed improves your efficiency in the water. A buoyancy aid is probably more comfortable for continuous wearing than a lifejacket.

A *Lifejacket* looks like a horse's collar and in Britain the best ones are manufactured to the British Standard Specification 3595 and are marked with the BSI 'kite-mark'. Lifejackets have to be designed to give greater safety than personal buoyancy aids. A lifejacket which conforms to BS 3595 will, when fully inflated, turn an unconscious person face upwards and float him on his back with mouth and nose clear of the water. There are several different types of lifejacket, some with built-in buoyancy and some which are blown up either by your own breath or using an automatic cylinder which provides gas inflation.

Boat safety

Always see that your dinghy carries the right safety equipment for your sailing water. The minimum for coastal use is one paddle (preferably two), a bucket, a proper anchor, a length of line attached to that anchor and to the boat and, if you are sailing without safety cover (i.e. rescue boats around you) smoke flares.

Left: A longjohn wetsuit with a bolero top, neoprene socks and a waterproof suit will keep you warm.

Until you gain more experience,* *don't* sail alone where nobody else can see you. If you do capsize, don't be tempted to swim away from your boat. It is much larger than you and will be seen more easily.

BOAT BUOYANCY

There are many different types of sailing dinghy,and modern designs have built-in buoyancy to make them unsinkable. The buoyancy takes the form of several sealed spaces at bow, stern or the sides of the boat. If water comes out of these tanks when the drain plug is removed, there may be structural damage, so check regularly.

Older boats may have buoyancy bags, usually made of a plastic material inflated by mouth or bellows. These are strapped firmly in position under the side benches or at bow and stern. A deflated bag clearly indicates a fault. The straps should be checked regularly, as they are subject to large loads when the dinghy is capsized. A buoyancy bag which floats away from a capsized dinghy does little for crew morale.

Some boats may have metal portable tanks secured under the side benches and foredeck, or solid buoyancy in the form of expanded polystyrene blocks. It is difficult to see if this type of buoyancy has soaked up water.

The amount of buoyancy in any dinghy is something which has already been decided for you by the builder, but some modern dinghies have so much buoyancy that they float high out of the water, making it difficult to reach the centreboard after a capsize. The distribution of buoyancy may also increase the tendency for a dinghy to invert completely. That is why you should use the more stable dinghies for your early sailing.

In distress or in need of assistance

There are 14 internationally recognised ways of signalling the fact that you are in distress and need assistance, but only two have any practical relevance to the dinghy sailor.

The first is to stand where you can be seen and raise and lower your arms, outstretched to each side, slowly and repeatedly.

The second is to use a distress flare. The best for dinghy use are the hand-held orange smoke flares with handle grips, and you should carry two of these whenever you are sailing a dinghy without safety cover in coastal waters. Modern flares are almost waterproof, but they should still be kept dry whenever possible. Don't stow them

in a buoyancy tank, or you may be unable to reach them if needed. Flares have a 'shelf-life' of three years, after which they must be replaced.

Read the firing instructions before you go afloat, so that you will know what to do in an emergency. Don't point the flare at anybody (including yourself) when you fire it, but hold it as high as you can and point it slightly downwind.

If you are not in distress, but merely want to attract attention, a whistle, wave or call to passing boats will be enough. The signals for distress must never be used when the occasion does not warrant them.

Below: If all else fails, use the international distress signal or let off an orange flare to attract attention.

THE HULL

The main part of the boat is the hull to which everything else is attached. It will normally be made of glass reinforced plastic (g.r.p) or wood.

THE RIG

The mast is normally left standing and is supported by three wires referred to collectively as the *standing rigging*. The wire to the front of the boat is the *forestay* and the wires to the sides are the *shrouds*. The screw fittings used to connect the wires to the boat are called *bottle screws*. When ropes are used instead they are called *lanyards*, and the fittings on the hull to which the shrouds are attached are *chainplates*.

SAILS

Most dinghy sails are triangular. The fore edge, attached to the forestay or mast, is the *luff*. It is secured to the *head*, and at the *tack* which is the bottom end of the luff. The free edge of the sail at the back is known as the *leech*, while the bottom of the sail is the *foot*. The point where they meet is the *clew*.

SAIL CONTROLS

Sails work only when they are set at a precise angle to the wind. They are raised by halyards and controlled by *sheets*. Their shape is controlled by lines such as *outhauls* and the *kicking strap vang*. All these ropes are termed collectively *running rigging*.

The kicking strap (vang) stops the boom lifting up when wind is in the sail, so maintaining the correct sail shape.

BOAT CONTROLS

A *centreboard* or daggerboard (an adjustable keel) is situated in the middle of a dinghy in a special housing. When sailing, it is lowered to prevent the hull sliding sideways through the water.

The *rudder* attached to the back of the boat is controlled by a *tiller* which usually has an extension to allow the person steering the boat to sit well forward.

Parts of the sail

Head
Batten
Leech
Luff
Mainsail
Clew   Foot   Tack
Head
Leech
Luff
Telltale
Clew
Foot   Tack
Jib

Parts of the boat

1	Hull
2	Mast
3	Boom
4	Forestay
5	Shrouds
6	Bottlescrews
7	Gooseneck
8	Mast step
9	Thwart
10	Centreboard c
11	Kicking strap
12	Toestraps
13	Mainsheet
14	Rudder
15	Tiller
16	Tiller extensio
17	Main traveller
18	Painter

Wind is made of moving air particles. When the particles hit a sail they bounce off, and in doing so give the sail a push. When the boat is running, with the wind behind her, that's what drives her along.

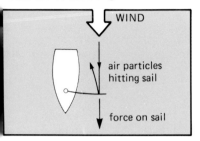

When the boat is sailing across the wind (reaching) or at an angle towards it (beating) the effect of the wind is more subtle. This is shown in the diagram below.

The air particles travel in a straight line if no force acts on them (1). As the wind moves over a curved sail the air particles follow the same curved path (2). They have to curve round the front, but they also curve round the back – if they didn't, a vacuum would be created behind the sail. The force which pulls the air particles in a curve round the back of the sail also acts on the sail

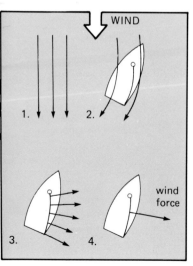

itself, pulling it in the opposite direction (note that, within reason, the bigger the curve in the sail, the greater the force). Because of the curve in the sail, the forces on each part develop in slightly different directions (3), but for convenience they can be represented as one force (4).

This force on the sail pulls the boat both forwards and sideways. The sideways force is largely resisted by the centreboard, which leaves the forward force to pull the boat through the water .

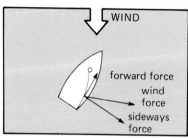

Where is the wind?

The wind is the source of your motive power when sailing, and it will have an influence on everything you do afloat. The helmsman sits with his back to the wind, the tiller held lightly in the hand nearest the stern, and the mainsheet in the forward hand. The crew sits further forward, adjusting his position to balance the boat.

The first indications of wind direction will be the feeling of the breeze on neck or ear, or from flags or smoke. Ripples will show on the water surface as the wind blows over it, and gusts can be spotted as the surface darkens with 'catspaws'.

The power of the sails is derived from the wind, but it will quickly become apparent that there is a limit beyond which no sail will work. When a sail is pointing directly into the wind, it will simply flap. To drive the boat along, the sails must be

kept at the correct angle to the wind. This basic principle governs much of what you do on the water.

When a sail is flapping, it is producing no driving force. As dinghies have no brakes, the way to stop is to let the sails flap by letting the sheets out. If the boat is pointing away from the wind, the rigging may prevent the sails from going right out, so you must turn the boat towards the wind.

Top: The classic helming position. Above: A boat will sail beautifully with the sail at the right angle to the wind. Let it out and the boat will stop.

The principal controls of a sailing dinghy are the tiller and the mainsheet, which are constantly adjusted while the boat is sailing.

Using the tiller

A boat is steered by her rudder, which is controlled by the tiller and the tiller extension.

The rudder will work only if there is a flow of water over it. When the helmsman moves the tiller off-centre, the rudder pushes the water to one side; in return the water pushes on the rudder and this push turns the boat.

Note that if you are sitting with your back to the wind and push on the tiller, the boat will always turn into the wind. If you pull the tiller towards you the boat turns away from the wind.

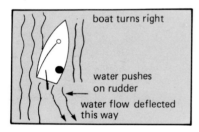

Controlling the mainsheet

Because the mainsheet is part of a pulley system, quite a lot of line needs to be pulled in or let out to adjust the boom. In the past sailors have used cleats (or their teeth) as an 'extra hand', but there is really no need. Take the tiller extension across your body, with the extension between your thumb and first finger; note you still have the rest of your hand to help with the sheets. In the photo sequence Ed Baird shows how useful this technique can be when winding in all the mainsheet as he heads up from a reach to a beat.

Above: Holding the tiller extension across your body lets you control the mainsheet with your tiller hand.

Top: The basic hove-to position. Above: To heave-to properly, you have to back the jib.

Heaving-to

By letting the tiller go when you let the sails flap, you will find that the boat looks after herself, coming to rest and sitting quietly in the water roughly at right angles to the wind. This is the basic hove-to position.

To heave-to properly 'back the jib' by pulling on the windward jibsheet to pull the sail to windward; this counteracts the effect of the mainsail. Push the tiller away from you to leeward, and raise the centreboard about a third. The result of all this is that the boat will make very little headway through the water. The actual sail positions vary from boat to boat but they are easy to work out by trial and error. Of course, you will never remain absolutely still in the water, or in relation to the land because, for one thing, the boat may be carried along by the tide.

From the *basic* hove-to position, you will find how, by pulling in on one sail or the other, you can cause the boat to turn into or away from the wind. You may also discover that heeling the boat one way or the other will affect its steering. Finally, by raising and lowering the centreboard you can see how the boat will tend to 'skid' across the water with no centreboard down. We'll now look at these effects in detail.

Sail setting

The rig of the typical two-man dinghy is designed such that the jib and mainsail work together to drive the boat forward. If from the basic hove-to position you pull in the jib, the boat will turn away from the wind and start to move forward. Similarly, if you pull in just the mainsail, the boat will turn into the wind and move forward. By sheeting both sails together, you'll get the boat moving most efficiently.

Above: To set a sail, let it out until it flaps (left), then haul in the sheet until the flapping stops (centre) and the telltales stream on both sides of the sail. If the leeward telltale is not streaming (right) the sail is hauled in too far.

As a general guide a sail, whether jib or main, will set best when it is let out until it starts to flap very gently along the luff, and is then pulled in just enough to stop the flapping. At this point there should be an even flow of air across both sides of the sail. This flow of air on the sail can be detected by the use of 'telltales', which are small lengths of wool sewn through the jib at three levels on the luff. Telltales on the main are attached to the leech.

Telltales are only aids to sail setting, as they merely indicate airflow over the part of the sail through which they are sewn, but they do show whether the airflow is smooth or stalled.

By trying to sail closer towards the wind, you will find that you have to pull the sails in harder, until you reach the stage when, even though they are pulled in tight, they still start to flap. This is the limit of windward sailing, the edge of the 'no-go zone' into which it is impossible to sail (see page 12).

Boat balance

As a general rule, dinghies sail fastest when they are upright. Considerable effort must be put in to achieving this, particularly when sailing in strong winds. You will often have to lean right out to windward, with your feet hooked under the toestraps. This is known as *hiking*.

When a dinghy is heeled to leeward, the most common situation in strong winds, the shape of the hull in the water becomes distorted, and tends to make the boat head up into the wind. The tiller has to be pulled to windward to keep the dinghy on a straight course (weather helm).

When a dinghy is heeled to

Above: Heeling to leeward (left) forces the sailor to pull hard on the tiller to keep the boat straight, while heeling to windward (above) has the opposite effect. Both slow you down.

windward the distortion of the shape at the waterline causes it to bear away from the wind. The tiller will have to be pushed to the leeward side of the dinghy to keep it on course (lee helm).

Another consequence of heeling is that the effective sail area presented to the wind is reduced, for the sail is diagonal to the wind instead of flat on.

Fore-and-aft trim

If the crew of a modern sailing dinghy sit forward in their boat the flat aft section of the hull is lifted out of the water. This reduces the wetted surface area (the amount of boat in contact with the water), cutting down friction and increasing boatspeed. This technique also

Above: Sit forward in light winds (top) to stop the stern dragging (centre). Sit aft in strong winds to lift the bows (bottom).

reduces leeway when sailing to windward.

In stronger winds, crew weight should be moved aft to lift the bow out of the water, so that the dinghy sails on its flat after sections. This will make the dinghy more stable and may encourage planing.

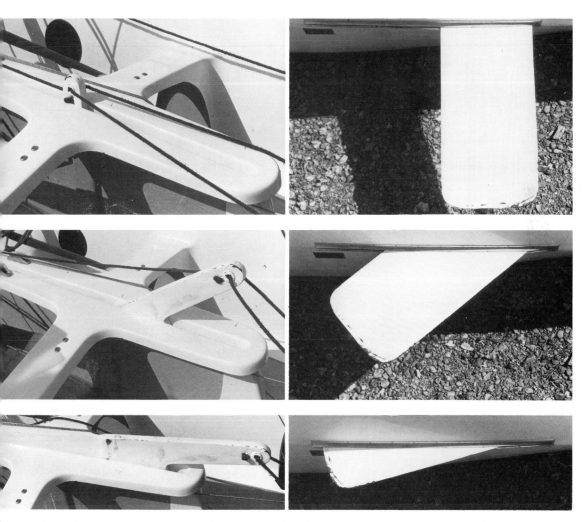

Centreboard position

As well as driving a dinghy forward, the action of the wind on the sails will push it sideways, across the water. This is described as *making leeway*. In order to prevent this, the dinghy needs more grip on the water, which is provided by a centreboard or daggerboard. The difference is simple. A centreboard pivots around a bolt in its case, while a daggerboard is moved vertically.

A boat makes most leeway when sailing close-hauled into the wind,

and so the centreboard should be right down. When sailing directly away from the wind there is no leeway, and so the board can be raised. In between, when sailing across the wind, the board should be half down. Many sailors mark either the board or the case as a guide and as you gain more experience you will be able to refine these basic rules for different conditions. The centreboard should be adjusted with every change of course to obtain the ideal compromise between excessive leeway and excessive drag. You

Above: The centreboard should be right down for beating (top), half down for reaching (centre) and well up for running (bottom).

should regard alterations of the centreboard position as an integral part of any change of course.

Even with the board right down, most dinghies will still make some leeway when close-hauled, particularly in waves. You must accept the fact that your actual destination will be slightly downwind of where the boat is pointing.

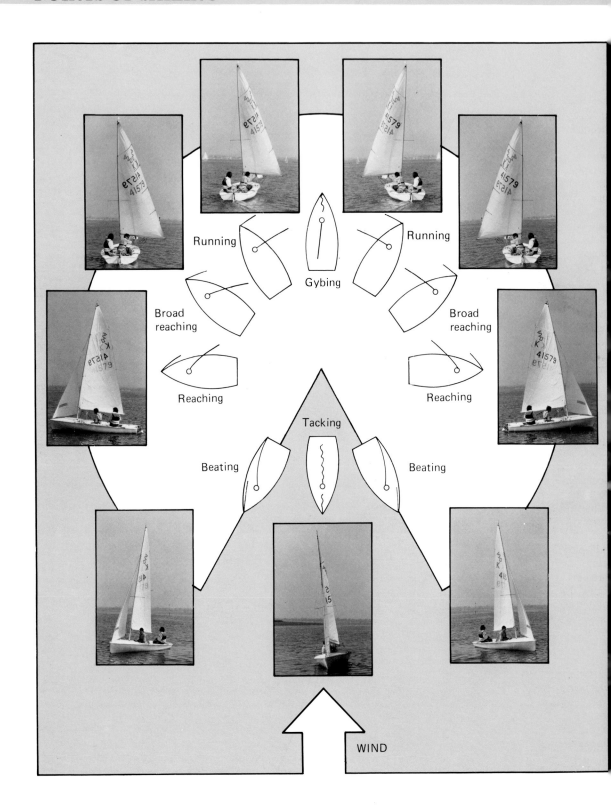

Running

Running

Gybing

Broad
reaching

Broad
reaching

Reaching

Reaching

Tacking

Beating

Beating

WIND

So far we have seen dealing with the theory of sailing, and in the next few pages we'll look at each point of sailing in detail. But first, let's simply go for a spin, without worrying too much about theory or style.

Before you set sail, tell someone where you're going and when you expect to return. (It's also polite to let them know you're back safely!). Just as important, pick the right place and conditions for your first sail. Wind is usually measured on the Beaufort scale: force 4 or above would be unsuitable.

A reservoir, river or estuary is a good place to learn to sail. If you are learning on the open sea, try to avoid a day with an offshore wind (wind blowing from shore to sea) – you may get blown a long way from shore. Always wear personal buoyancy and stay with the boat.

Find where the wind is coming from by looking at smoke, flags, your boat's burgee or the waves. Then pick a goal that will involve sailing at right angles to the wind (Goal 1).

Your objective is simple: to rig the boat, launch her and sail towards your goal for a short distance. Then turn the boat round, with the bow passing 'through' the wind, and sail back to your starting point. Easy!

If you'd like to do a bit more, turn round again, with the bow passing through the wind as before, and repeat the process until you feel fairly confident. Then try steering for a goal that is slightly to windward (Goal 2), before returning to your starting point.

You will need to sit on the windward side of the boat – that is, with your back to the wind. Your crew should sit in a position which keeps the boat level. Hold the tiller in your aft (back) hand and the mainsheet in your forward (front) hand. When you turn round you will need to swap hands.

Wind force		
	At sea	On land
0	Sea like a mirror	Calm; smoke rises vertically
1	Ripples	Smoke drifts; wind vanes not affected
2	Small wavelets	Wind felt on face; leaves rustle
3	Large wavelets; crests begin to break	Leaves and small twigs in constant motion; Wind extends light flags
4	Small waves becoming longer; fairly frequent white horses	Raises dust and loose paper; small branches are moved
5	Moderate waves; many white horses; some spray	Small trees in leaf begin to sway

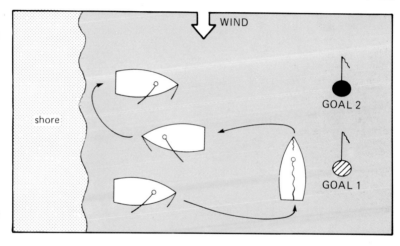

As you steer the boat, experiment by pushing the tiller away and pulling it towards you. You'll soon learn its effect: pushing on the tiller turns the bow into the wind, pulling it back makes the bow turn away from the wind. Then try to keep the boat on a straight course: don't grip the tiller – use it gently but firmly to make the boat do what you want.

The sheets control the sails, and in particular how much of the wind's power they are using. For this exercise the sails will be about half-way out. If a gust comes along, keep steering in a straight line and slacken the sheets, letting the sails out a bit to spill some of the wind. Let them out as much as necessary to prevent excessive heel. When the gust has passed pull in the sheets again to fill the sails with wind. If you get out of control, let go of the sheets altogether.

Sail controls

An expert constantly adjusts the various sail controls to set his sails to the best advantage, but the beginner has other things to worry about. For the present make sure the halyards and kicking strap (vang) are tight. The main outhaul should be set so there is a reasonable curve in the front of the sail. Then leave these controls alone, and concentrate on adjusting the sheets and centreboard.

Reaching, or sailing across the wind, is probably the easiest point of sailing. It's also the fastest!

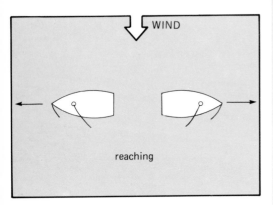

reaching

Adjusting the sail

The secret of reaching is sail trim. Pick a goal and steer a straight course towards it. Let each sail out until the front begins to flap. Then pull in the sails until they just stop flapping.

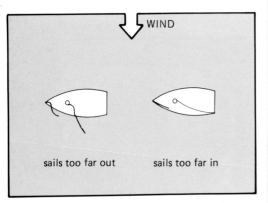

sails too far out   sails too far in

The wind changes in strength and direction every few seconds, so the sails must be trimmed constantly. Keep the sheets in your hands all the time, and let them out every few moments to try to increase drive. If

Right: Good reaching technique: the boat is level and the sail well out.

Left: Excessive heel slows you down: this helmsman should hike out.
Below: This sail is pulled in too far for efficiency on a reach.

the sails flap they are too far out. If the boat heels over and slows down, the sails are too far in.

When you turn slightly closer to the wind, you'll find that the sails will flap, so you'll need to pull in the sheets gently, a correction which will soon become automatic. When you bear away from the wind, however, there is no simple sign to remind you to ease the sheets. In fact the most common beginner's mistake is forgetting to ease sheets when bearing away.

Steering

Try to keep a reasonably straight course: each time you change direction you will have to adjust the sail. If there is a strong 'pull' on the tiller extension, it's usually because the boat is heeling over too much. Ease sheets or hike out to bring the boat level; the pull will disappear and you can then steer easily.

Trim

You should normally sit in the middle of the windward deck when reaching. This ensures that the best hull shape is presented to the water. Move forward in light winds to reduce the amount of hull skin in the water (and so reduce skin friction). Move aft in strong winds to lift the bow and help the boat to plane.

Centreboard

Have the centreboard half up, to reduce drag and make the boat easier to handle. If you want to change course closer to the wind, push the centreboard down slightly; pull it up a little if you change course away from the wind.

Gusts

Look over your shoulder occasionally to see if a gust is coming. The water looks dark as a gust travels over it.

When the gust hits, hike out. If the boat still heels over, let the sheets out until the boat comes level. Don't forget to pull the sheets back in again as the gust passes, or the boat will try to capsize on top of you!

Don't let the gust turn the boat round into the wind. Be firm with the tiller and keep the boat going in the direction you want.

Light winds

Reaching in light winds needs patience. Try to keep still – if the boat rocks about the wind will be 'shaken' out of the sails.

Sit a little further forward than usual, and heel the boat to leeward. This helps the sails hang in the right shape. Easing the sail controls – halyards, kicking strap (vang) and outhaul – will give more power.

Strong winds

When reaching in strong winds sit further aft to lift the bows, and with luck the boat will plane like a speedboat over the water – the ultimate sailing experience!

Keep a good grip on the tiller extension. If the boat heels hike out; if you're still overpowered turn into the wind slightly and let out the sails a little. By constantly adjusting the sheets and tiller you can keep the boat on her feet and let her go really fast. If you are still having problems the sail controls may be too loose; tighten them all, particularly the kicking strap (vang) and the outhaul. The sails produce less power when stretched out in this way.

If there are waves, use them. As each wave picks up the boat turn away from the wind and pull in the sheets to promote surfing.

Above: Reaching in strong winds the boat will plane across the surface at high speed. Good boat balance is essential: here the crew is using a trapeze to get his weight as far outboard as possible.

Opposite: This sail is too far out, as shown by the flapping luff. Pull in the mainsheet!

The satisfaction which comes from efficient beating is tremendous. You are, literally, beating the wind which is trying to push you back.

What is beating?

You cannot sail a straight course directly into the wind. If you try, you'll find the sails will flap and the boat will stop. Your only option is to sail a zigzag course towards your destination, with each 'zig' at about 45 degrees to the wind.

Steering

From a reach, turn gently towards the wind. You will need to pull in the sails as you turn, or they will flap. You must also lower the centreboard fully or the dinghy will slip sideways through the water.

Eventually you will have turned so far that the sails are pulled right in. In most boats this will put you on a course of about 45 degrees to the wind. If you try to turn further into the wind the jib begins to flap along the leading edge (luff). You are, in fact, entering the 'no-go zone' (see page 12), so pull the tiller towards you and turn back until the jib fills.

Keep adjusting your course: turn towards the wind until the front of the jib begins to flap, and the boat stops trying the heel and begins to slow down; then turn away from the wind until the jib fills and she picks up speed. You should repeat this every few seconds, because the wind constantly changes its direction.

Every so often turn 90 degrees through the wind (tack) to make the classic zig-zag course to windward.

Right: Beating on starboard tack (top), through the eye of the wind (centre) onto port tack (bottom).

Trim

Sit fairly well forward unless the boat is crashing into the waves, in which case move back to let the bow ride over them. If the wind is at all strong both you and your crew should be on the windward deck to counteract the large heeling forces experienced when beating.

Centreboard

The centreboard should be right down, although in very strong winds it may pay to raise the board a little to make the steering lighter.

Gusts

The water looks dark as a gust travels over it. As a gust hits you, hike out hard and turn into the wind a few degrees. If the boat still heels, let the sails out a little. When the boat has picked up speed, pull the sails in again. When the gust has passed, move your weight inboard and adjust your course

Sail controls

The jib luff (the front edge of the sail), is your reference point for beating. Unless the luff is straight it's difficult to assess how close to the wind you're sailing, so pull the jib halyard reasonably tight to take out any creases or 'scallops' in the sail.

Pull the jibsheet in firmly, but not so tight as to take the shape (belly) out of the sail.

The mainsheet should be pulled in firmly for medium winds, but let out a little in strong or in light airs. Pull on the cunningham to take the creases out of the front of the sail. Pull the kicking strap (vang) on harder as the wind increases, to stop the boom rising.

Below: Keep the boat upright on the beat and you will sail faster.

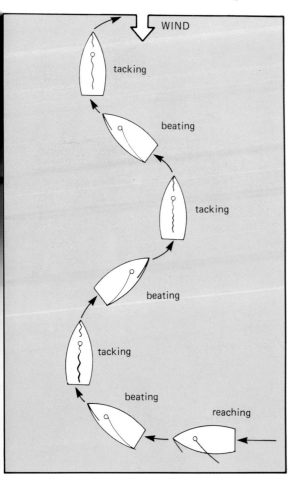

Light winds

Aim for speed rather than steering very close to the wind. Keep an eye on the water and on your burgee to spot windshifts. Sit forward and if necessary heel the boat to leeward. Both actions cut down the wetted areas of the hull, and heeling will make the sail fall into a good aerofoil shape. You may need a long tiller extension if you are to get right forward.

Strong winds

In these conditions both the wind and the waves tend to stop the boat. You must not let this happen because you can only steer when the boat is moving – so speed through the waves is your main aim.

Let out the sheets a little and 'feather' the boat into gusts. Don't worry if the front part of each sail flaps – you won't be able to handle full sail anyway.

Try to steer so the boat has an easy passage over the waves. As the bow goes up a wave, push the tiller away a little. Pull the tiller back as the bow reaches the crest, and turn away down the back of the wave. Repeat this for each wave – you will find you're moving all the time.

Your body weight provides the power to get to windward. The more you hike, the faster you go. Adjust the toe strap so you're comfortable. If you trail in the water, or if your shins hurt, tighten the toe strap; otherwise, loosen it so you can get further outboard.

Sail controls

The kicking strap (vang), and the cunningham, outhaul and jib halyard should all be bar tight.

Above: If you get it right you can sail really fast on the beat.
Facing page: Some common mistakes. (Top left) The sail controls are too loose. Note the curve in the kicking strap (vang) which should be tight, and the creases halfway up the sail. (Top right) This boat is heeling too much; this makes the hull shape inefficient and slows it down. (Bottom left) Steering too far off the wind will make the boat heel. The helmsman should alter course or let the sail out. (Bottom right) Steering too close to the wind makes the front of the sail flap and reduces power dramatically.

Tacking is an integral part of sailing to windward. You also need to tack to turn round and to avoid large objects. Later on, you will tack on windshifts when you're racing. In short, the ability to tack efficiently will stand you in good stead throughout your sailing life.

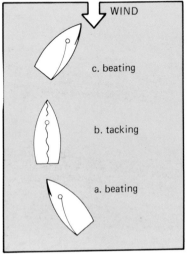

c. beating

b. tacking

a. beating

The basic manoeuvre

The boat in the diagram is beating with the wind on the starboard side (a). The boat turns into the wind (b), and keeps turning until it is beating with the wind on the port side (c). The turn is called a tack.

The tacking manoeuvre requires coordination of feet, hands and body to make a smooth, efficient turn. It's well worth practising the technique on land before you go afloat for the first time.

There is a big difference between tacking a boat with a centre mainsheet (where the mainsheet comes to your hand from the middle of the cockpit) and tacking a boat with a stern mainsheet. We'll look at them both here.

Tacking – centre mainsheet

In a centre-mainsheet dinghy, the tacking procedure is as follows:
● Helm checks to windward. If clear, calls 'ready about'. Crew unjams the jibsheet, helm unjams the mainsheet.

● Crew answers 'yes'. Helm begins to move in and eases the mainsheet. If Crew is on a trapeze, he moves inboard and unhooks.

● Helm calls 'lee oh', puts his aft foot across the boat and pushes the tiller hard away. As the boom comes across, he moves towards the

middle of the boat, aft foot first, facing forward. Crew starts to move across.

● Helm revolves the tiller extension forward around the end of the tiller, moving across the boat and holding the mainsheet. Crew changes sheets and moves across to the other side of the boat.

● As the sails fill again, Helm sits down on the new side steering with his tiller arm behind his back, then brings his sheet hand across in front of his body to hold both the tiller and sheet. Crew prepares to go out on the trapeze, if fitted.

Above: Tacking, centre mainsheet.

● Helm releases the tiller from his 'old' tiller hand and takes the mainsheet in that hand. Crew sheets in the jib, and Helm centralises the tiller. Both adjust balance, trim and sheets for the new course.

Tacking – aft mainsheet

The technique of tacking an aft-mainsheet dinghy is somewhat different, although the end result should be the same – a smooth transition from one tack to the other:

- Helm sits well forward of the tiller, front hand holding the mainsheet, rear hand holding the end of the tiller extension (palm up, thumb on top). Spare mainsheet is tucked well under the tiller.
- Helm checks area, then calls, 'ready about'. Crew then checks and (if clear) answers 'yes'. Helm clips the mainsheet under his thumb, and pushes the tiller away from him with his back hand, saying 'lee oh' as he does it.
- As the boom reaches the quarter, Crew releases the jib. Helm begins to move across the boat, facing aft, and puts his free hand on the tiller extension, close to (and behind) the other hand, with the thumb on top pointing towards the tiller.
- Helm keeps the tiller hard over and revolves the tiller extension around and forward as he moves across the boat. Crew picks up the new jibsheet and balances the boat.
- When the boom reaches the new quarter both sit down.
- Helm centralises the tiller and Crew sheets in the jib.
- Helm and Crew trim the sails and adjust the trim.

Left: World champion helmsman Lawrie Smith shows how it's done in a centre-mainsheet Fireball. Note the way he handles the tiller.

Above: Tacking an aft-mainsheet dinghy. The helmsman faces aft as he moves across; in a centre-mainsheet boat he faces forward.

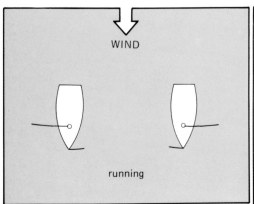

running

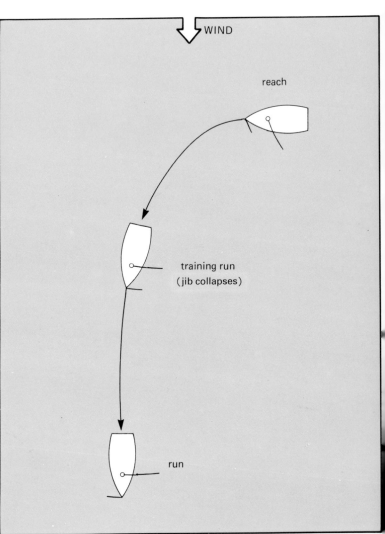

Running is sailing with the wind directly behind the boat, as shown in the diagram. To move from a reach to a run pull the tiller *gently* towards you, and pay out the sheets. Aim to bear away (turn from the wind) in a gentle arc. You'll need less centreboard, but don't raise it completely: leave a little down to give a bit of grip on the water. Now you're sailing downwind or *running*.

If you sail directly away from the wind there's a danger that a small change in wind direction could cause an unexpected gybe – the wind fills the wrong side of the mainsail and causes the boom to swing violently from one side of the boat to the other. To avoid this start your downwind sailing by adopting what is known as the training run: just a few degrees off a dead downwind course. You'll know that you've borne away sufficiently because the jib will go limp, hanging in the windshadow of the mainsail.

On a run, avoid violent turns – if the boat is travelling fast the centrifugal force may capsize you.

When you have a little more experience and want to sail dead downwind, the boat will go faster and be slightly more stable if you goosewing the jib – that is, pull it out to windward where it will fill cleanly, unhampered by the blanketing effect of the mainsail.

Trim

Except in light winds, sit towards the back of the cockpit. The wind tends to push the bow down on a run, and your weight near the stern helps counteract this.

There is no need to hike on a run. Sit near the centreline and be ready to move your weight either way. Watch out that the tiller doesn't catch on your thigh; think ahead so you don't have to make violent tiller movements.

Adjusting the mainsheet

In medium and light winds the mainsheet should be as far out as possible. In strong winds, when the boat tends to roll, pull the mainsheet in a little – but remember that the boat goes fastest with the sail right out. Don't forget to tie a knot in the end of the mainsheet!

Right: Running dead downwind, with the mainsail right out and the jib goosewinged.

Centreboard

Pull the centreboard well up. In very strong winds, however, leave the centreboard about half down to dampen rolling. Never have the centreboard right down when running, and never take a daggerboard out – this creates too much turbulence in the slot.

Gusts

Keep going, even in strong gusts. Don't let the gust turn the boat round into the wind – keep a straight course. If the boat heels away from you, let the mainsheet out. If it heels towards you, pull the mainsheet in.

Sail controls

You can safely leave the sail controls alone on a run. But if you want to go a little faster make the sails baggy by letting off the halyards and cunningham and easing the kicking strap (vang) until the top batten is in line with the boom.

Light winds

Sit as far forward as you can, holding the boom out. In very light winds, heel the boat to leeward to help keep the boom out and to put some shape in the sail. Use the tiller as little as possible, because it only acts as a brake.

Above: Good running style. The centreboard is up, the sail is well out, and the kicking strap (vang) is tight. The helmsman is sitting well back to make the bow lift.

Strong winds

Don't be in a hurry to get on a run when the wind is really blowing. Steer round gradually from a reach, letting the sail out slowly as you do do. Move back in the boat to help the bow lift.

As you come on to the run, the boat will move really fast. If it starts to roll, immediately pull the mainsheet in a little. Keep a firm hand on the tiller, and don't let the boat turn back onto a reach. On the

other hand, don't turn so far that you risk gybing.

Try to sail down the waves. As a wave comes up behind turn away from the wind and surf on the wave. If you shoot down it and the bow looks as though it's going to hit the wave in front, turn into the wind a little and try to climb the new wave. If you're overtaking the waves, you're really going fast!

ADJUSTING THE SAIL

Keep the mainsheet as far out as possible without allowing the boat to roll. It may help to move the knot in the mainsheet to keep it in this position. Then, if you accidentally let go of the mainsheet all *may* not be lost.

'Play' the mainsheet. If the boat heels towards you, pull the mainsheet in; let it out if the boat heels away from you. Try to avoid violent movements.

Keep the centreboard half down, and make sure all the sail controls are tight.

Above left: If the boat heels to leeward, let out the mainsheet.
Above right: If it heels to windward, pull in the mainsheet. This Laser sailor may have left it too late!

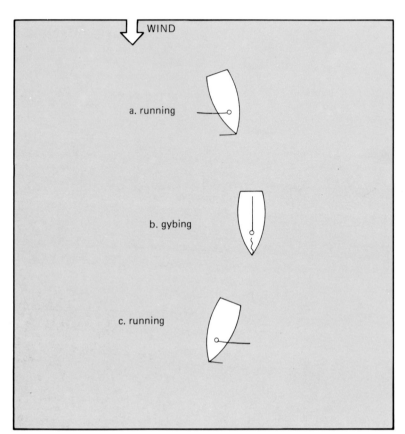

WIND

a. running

b. gybing

c. running

In the diagram, boat (a) is running with the mainsail on the starboard side. The helmsman turns through a small angle (b). The wind forces the mainsail out to the port side of the boat (c). The manoeuvre is called a *gybe*.

Unlike tacking, the wind is pushing on the sail throughout the gybe. The boat is moving at high speed, so it is very sensitive to tiller movements. A miscalculation results in the boat rolling – with the sails 'edge on' there's not much to dampen the roll and you tend to take an involuntary dip.

Decide when you want to gybe, and then do it! The best moment is when the boat is moving fast down a wave – since you're travelling away the wind, the 'push' on the sail is reduced.

Centreboard

It is absolutely vital to pull the centreboard up most of the way before you begin a gybe. If you gybe with the centreboard down the board locks the bottom of the boat in the water and provides a pivot point for the wind to lever the boat onto her side. With the board up, if anything goes wrong the boat simply skids sideways. However, take care with a daggerboard: on some boats it may foul the kicking strap (vang) when pulled fully up, with spectacular results.

Strong winds

In very strong winds a capsize may be inevitable. If you can't pull in the mainsheet on the run, it's better to *wear round*. This involves turning through 360 degrees, tacking half-way round. Do this with the centreboard half down. Pull in the mainsheet and spin around fast.

Gybing – centre mainsheet

As with tacking, the technique of gybing differs according to the mainsheet rig. With a centre-mainsheet dinghy the procedure is as follows:

- Helm balances the boat as necessary and checks all round – especially the area into which the boat is turning. He holds the extension in a 'dagger' grip. Calling 'stand by to gybe', he cleats the mainsheet.
- Helm revolves the extension over to the new side without altering the tiller itself, and steps (back foot first) into the middle of the boat. Crew also places his back foot across the boat.
- Helm changes hands on the tiller extension (behind his back).

The old tiller hand takes the falls of the mainsheet. Crew moves into the centre of the boat and changes jib sheets.
- Helm calls 'gybe oh', pushes the tiller towards his original sitting position and helps the boom across.
- As soon as the boom starts to move, Helm centralises the tiller sharply, takes up the mainsheet with the 'falls hand' and sits down on the new windward side.
- Helm trims the mainsheet and settles down to the new course. Crew trims jibsheet.

As you gain experience you will be able to gybe with the mainsheet and extension in the 'old' hands. Then you only change hands when you're safely installed on the new side deck.

Above: Gybing a centre-mainsheet dinghy in light airs.

Gybing – aft mainsheet

● Helm sits forward of the tiller, and puts the boat on a training run. He checks that the centreboard is only slightly down, checks around, especially the area to leeward and says 'stand by to gybe'. Crew checks the area and says, 'yes'.

● Helm pulls in the mainsheet to bring the boom off the shroud. He clips the mainsheet under his thumb, putting spare down behind the extension.

● Helm puts his free hand onto the extension close to the other hand, thumb on top pointing towards the tiller, and separates the mainsheet into the other hand by rolling his wrist outwards. Saying 'gybe-oh' he moves to the middle of the boat, taking the extension round and forward to the other side. He then initiates the gybe by pushing the extension towards where he was sitting and waits for the boom to swing across. Crew changes jib sheets and moves to the centre of the boat.

● As the mainsail clew lifts Helm quickly centralises the tiller so that his weight, boom and tiller are simultaneously in the middle of the boat.

● Helm sits out on the new windward side and keeps a good lookout. Crew balances the boat and sets the jib once it has changed sides.

Above and right: Gybing an aft-mainsheet dinghy. Remember to duck as the boom swings across!

When you watch experts sailing, it is obvious that they know when the boat is going to capsize. Moving quickly, they are over the windward side and onto the centreboard before the mast touches the water. For such sailors, righting a capsized dinghy is second nature, and although it may be some time before *you* are sailing a high-performance dinghy in a high wind, as a beginner you must know how to recover after a capsize.

A capsize is most likely to happen when you don't react quickly enough to a gust. Before you know it, the dinghy has heeled right over until the sail hits the water and you fall out.

The golden rule is *stay with the boat*. Even if you cannot get sailing again, don't be tempted to swim for the shore. The boat's inherent buoyancy will keep you afloat and out of the water, and it's much easier for others to see a capsized dinghy than a head in the water.

Righting the boat

● Both the crew swim to the stern and Helm checks that the rudder is secure. Crew finds the end of the mainsheet and gives it to Helm who, using it as a lifeline, swims around the outside of the boat to the centreboard. Crew swims along the inside of the boat to the centreboard case.
● Crew checks that the centreboard is fully down and Helm holds on to it to prevent the boat inverting. Meanwhile Crew finds the top (weather) jib sheet and throws it over to Helm.

● Crew lies in the hull facing forward and floats above the submerged side-deck *without hanging on to the boat*. The extra weight won't help Helm and may make it impossible for him to right the dinghy.
● Helm climbs on to the centreboard, keeping his weight as close to the hull as possible to avoid breaking the board. Then he hauls on the jib sheet and rights the boat with Crew in it.
● With the jib backed the dinghy is hove-to, and Crew is then able to help Helm aboard. In fact, Helm may be able to get half-way into the boat as it comes upright.

Some modern dinghies have the buoyancy distributed in such a way that they tend to turn upside-down immediately. To counteract this you should never hang onto the inside of

the dinghy as it capsizes but simply drop into the water. If the dinghy does invert, the easiest way to get it back on its side – providing the mast has not stuck in the mud at the bottom – is for the crew to press down on one side of the stern, while the helmsman uses his weight and leverage on the centreboard. Once the dinghy is lying on its side, proceed as before.

RIGHTING SINGLEHANDERS
If the dinghy capsizes to leeward, climb over the edge of the hull and stand on the daggerboard where it emerges from the hull. Hold on to the gunwhale, lean back and slowly pull the boat upright.

In a windward capsize you may be thrown out before the boat stops. Hold on to the mainsheet if possible, swim to the boat and hang on to the daggerboard. Your weight on the daggerboard may be enough to lift the mast and sail clear of the water, when the wind will take over and flip the boat upright. If not, climb on to the daggerboard and pull gently on the hull to lift the mast just clear of the water. The wind will then push the boat around until the sail is downwind, when you can continue as outlined above.

If the dinghy inverts, pull the daggerboard as far out as possible. You might be able to right it by standing on the *windward* gunwhale, holding on to the daggerboard and leaning back.

Bailing

Modern dinghies will come upright with so little water aboard that you can sail on immediately, using the self-bailers in the bottom of the hull as soon as you pick up speed.

Many older dinghies will come up full of water, which must be bailed out. If the water level is above the top of the centreboard case you will have to work fast, or you will be fighting a losing battle as water comes in through the centreboard slot. It should be clear that a bailer is an essential part of the dinghy's equipment. The worst bailer is the one which floats away from the capsized boat, so make sure it is tied on.

Above: Righting a capsized two-handed dinghy from a near-inverted position. Note how the crew is scooped aboard as the boat comes upright again.
Below: Righting a singlehander that has capsized to windward.

Reefing is the process of reducing sail so you have the right amount for the prevailing conditions. It is always easier to reef ashore before setting out and, if necessary, shake out the reef.

Aft-mainsheet dinghies usually have roller reefing. To reduce sail, loosen the main halyard to lower the sail, unclip the kicking strap (vang) and lift the boom off the mast fitting. Then roll the sail on to the boom, taking a tuck at the clew and stretching the sail towards the end so the boom doesn't droop. Make sure there are no wrinkles. When sufficient sail has been rolled on, re-attach the boom to the mast fitting and take up the main halyard. During the final rolls it is usual to roll in the sail bag or something similar with the rope hanging out so that you can re-attach the kicking strap (vang), for the original fitting will have disappeared into the roll of the sail. This is called a reefing strop.

Points reefing

Some older dinghies have points reefing. Lines of small strings (reefing points) are sewn into sail on either side at intervals. To 'take down' your first reef, take the front reefing point (the tack pennant) and make it fast, then the rear reefing point (the clew pennant) and form a new foot to the sail. You will be left with a 'bag' of loose sail which you roll up neatly and tie (not too tightly) with reef knots using the small reefing points.

Centre-mainsheet dinghies

Normal roller reefing is impossible if the mainsheet blocks are attached to the centre of the boom. If the dinghy has an unstayed mast the sail may be rolled round the mast. If not,

reefing may not be practicable, unless the dinghy is equipped with points reefing or its modern equivalent, slab reefing.

When to reef

If the wind falls light you can easily shake out a reef. It is far more difficult and dangerous to put in a reef when you are actually sailing and the wind increases. With some dinghies, it is necessary to reef the jib or drop it completely when you reef the mainsail, in order to maintain the right balance of sail area.

There are, however, times when you will need to reef afloat. Choose a suitable place. If you can pick up a mooring or drop anchor, this may make the whole operation easier. If neither is possible, make sure that there is plenty of searoom to leeward so that the boat doesn't drift ashore.

On this occasion heave to. The *basic* hove-to position is not adequate. You should, preferably, be on the starboard tack in order to keep the right of way (see page 38). For aft-mainsheet dinghies, the procedure is as follows:
- Lower half the mainsail.
- Remove the kicking strap.
- With one person at the tack of the mainsail and the other at the clew, take a tuck of about 18 inches (50cm) out of the leech of the sail and roll it round the boom, keeping the sail well pulled towards the boom end.
- Remove the bottom batten.
- Roll in a reefing strop.
- With this in position rotate the boom to roll the sail around it. Take about four turns.
- Having rolled up the sail, replace the boom, tack downhaul, outhaul and kicker (vang) and sail away.

Left: Reefing an aft-mainsheet dinghy while hove-to.

If one of the crew falls overboard the remaining crew must be able to turn the boat round and return to the same spot as quickly as possible. There are many ways of doing this, but the following is a sound method of returning, singlehanded and in full control. In a dinghy, it is possible that you will first have to right the craft, since the sudden loss of crew weight may well cause a capsize.

Assuming that you can sail on: gain control and sail off on a beam reach, letting the jib fly. Keep an eye on the person in the water, who should, if possible, hold up a hand and shout to keep in touch.

When you are at least ten lengths away, tack (don't gybe) onto a reciprocal course, and go back the way you came. As you get nearer to the casualty sail on a broad reach well to leeward of him to give yourself room to turn up on to a close reach: when you get level you can ease the mainsheet and stop dead beside him. As you move forward, flick the tiller to windward and position yourself just behind the windward shroud. The boat will be hove-to with sails flapping.

The only difficult part of the manoeuvre is the judgement of boat speed on your final approach. Practise it often.

Hauling someone aboard can present problems. It sometimes helps to rock the boat so that the gunwhale is immersed as the person is pulled in. Don't try hauling him in over the transom. The boat automatically bears away and begins to sail off out of control. The tiller is easily damaged; and worse still, it is not pleasant to be dragged over a gadget-cluttered transom.

If the casualty is exhausted, or injured, it is easier to haul aboard one part of the body at a time, taking care to secure it, rather than try to lift the whole body. As a last resort, you may have to capsize the dinghy, secure the man to the thwart or seat and 'scoop' him aboard.

Below: Practising the man overboard routine.

As with every other form of transport there are accepted rules governing what you should or should not be doing when you are sailing near other boats.

In general, as a beginner it is always better to slow or stop the boat by letting the sails go and pointing it into the wind, rather than turn the boat away from the wind causing it to gain momentum. If you hit anything at speed you will cause considerably more damage than if the boat is slowing down and stopping.

Meeting power boats

If you have grown up believing that power boats give way to sailing boats, beware! Such a rule applies in open water, but in rivers and estuaries large ships must keep to dredged channels or they will run aground. Consequently *they* have the right of way and you must take care not to impede their progress. However, small powered boats which are not restricted in their movements should give way to sail, because it is easier for them to stop or change course.

Channels

In a channel marked by buoys or stakes you should keep to the *right*. This presents problems when the wind is against you, but you will soon learn how to 'short tack' keeping to the correct side of the channel.

Overtaking

Overtaking vessels must keep clear of the vessels being overtaken.

Meeting other sailing boats

For the purposes of the rules, boats are said to be on port tack or starboard tack depending on whether the wind is blowing onto the port or starboard side of the boat.

Looking from the stern towards the bow, the port side is *left* and the starboard side is *right*. If you are in any doubt write PORT and STARBOARD on the sides of the boom.

When boats are on opposite tacks, those on starboard tack have right of way over those on port tack, so if you have the wind blowing over the port side, keep out of the way of boats on starboard tack. If it takes you some time to work out which tack an approaching boat is on, tack away from it just to be on the safe side.

Boats on starboard tack have a duty to maintain their course and heading while other boats are giving way to them. So if you are on starboard tack, keep going unless it becomes clear that the other boat is not going to give way.

When boats are travelling together or converging on the same tack, the boat which is closest to the wind (windward boat) must keep out of the way of the leeward boat.

Signifying your intentions

If there is the slightest risk of collision take avoiding action and signify your intentions in plenty of time. It is important that the avoiding action is obvious to the other vessel, so be definite, and do whatever you intend to do in ample time.

Above: One of the basic rules of the road – the Laser (123456) is on port tack and must keep clear of the starboard tack dinghy.

Above: This time the Laser has right of way – when both are on the same tack the windward boat must keep clear of the leeward boat.

If your sailing dinghy is kept on a mooring you will have to get to it somehow. The usual way is to row out in a small boat. Indeed almost everyone who is starting to sail will have to handle a boat under oars at some time and it is worth remembering a few basic rules.

First, when you get into any dinghy, step carefully into the centre and sit down quickly. Those who jump or stand on the edge of the boat reap their own reward.

See to it that the load (gear or passengers) is distributed evenly. If there are two of you it is much easier if one rows and the other sits at the stern of the boat. If your passenger sits in the bows they dig

into the water, making the boat difficult to row.

Once in the boat put the rowlocks (crutches) in position and then insert the oars as you push off.

As you come alongside a quay or another boat, approach into the tide or current because this will slow you down. Remove the nearside oar first so that it doesn't get trapped or broken. Obviously you must hold on to the quay or whatever while you stow both the oars and your rowlocks, and when you climb out of the dingy remember to take the painter (mooring line) with you. If you forget you will lose your dinghy. Remember also that a rowing dinghy (especially a rubber one) is

affected by wind and tide and you will sometimes find it difficult to row against both.

When you secure the dinghy you must allow for the tide if you are going to leave it at a quay for some time. If the tide is rising it may get trapped under the quay if it is on too long a line, and if the tide is falling and the line is too short the dinghy may finish up suspended clear of the water!

Below, top row: Step onto the centreline of the rowing dinghy, and arrange crew weight evenly. Bottom row: As you approach, take out the nearest oar. Finally step onto the centreline of the sailing dinghy.

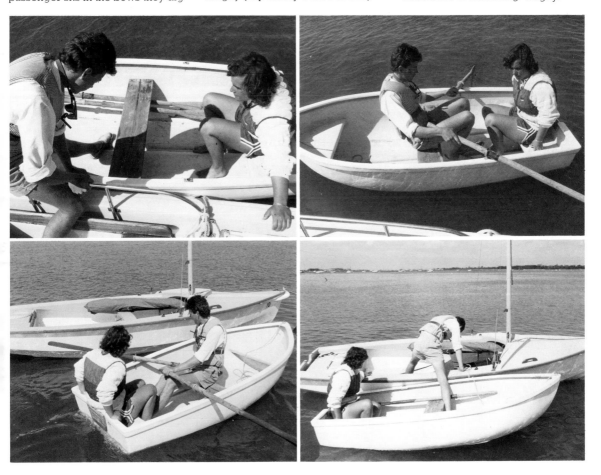

The majority of damage to sailing dinghies is caused when they are being launched and recovered. Great care must be taken to ensure that the hull does not come into contact with the beach. This means that at least one member of the crew must be prepared to get wet. Thorough preparation before launching is also essential. The sails should be rigged and the boat securely attached to its trolley with a suitable quick-release knot. All the gear should be checked before going near the water. Bear the following points in mind:

- Never step into a boat on dry land. When the bottom of the boat is not supported by water the pressure of your foot may be sufficient to make a hole.
- When moving a dinghy on a trolley make sure that you tie the bow down to the trolley handle (using the painter). If the rudder is attached, check that the rudder blade has been pulled up and secured.
- When launching the dinghy from a trolley push the trolley right down so that the dinghy will float off freely.
- Make sure that the trolley is parked out of other people's way and above the high-water mark.
- When you return, immerse the trolley deep into the water and pull the dinghy over it by the painter. Do not drag the boat onto the trolley or you will damage its bottom.

Launching in an onshore wind

In strong winds the more help that can be found to launch the boat the easier it will be. Substantial damage can be caused by waves dropping the boat on its trolley or on to the beach. A number of people lifting the boat into deep water will

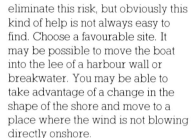

eliminate this risk, but obviously this kind of help is not always easy to find. Choose a favourable site. It may be possible to move the boat into the lee of a harbour wall or breakwater. You may be able to take advantage of a change in the shape of the shore and move to a place where the wind is not blowing directly onshore.

- Assess the wave pattern and choose the best tack on which to leave the shore, to get through the waves as nearly as possible at right angles.
- Take the boat bow first on its trolley into the water, having first secured the bow to the trolley with only a round turn, or slip knot.
- Float the boat on a suitable wave and pull it clear of the trolley as fast as possible.
- With the boat clear, retrieve the trolley.
- Crew holds the boat in deep water head to wind.
- Helmsman hoists the sails, fixes the rudder and lowers the centreboard halfway.
- Crew holds the bow of the boat so that it is pointing on the appropriate tack.
- Helmsman sheets in the main; crew pushes the bow in the correct direction and climbs in on the windward side.
- As the boat leaves the shore lower more centreboard and, once clear of the shore, pull in the jib. Check that the rudder downhaul is cleated. It may pay to row or paddle the boat off a lee shore. This is usually advantageous when the dinghy can be rowed to a suitable mooring. Then the sails can be hoisted.

Landing in an onshore wind

The easiest way to land in an onshore wind is to turn the boat head up wind some way off, drop the main and sail to the beach under jib alone:

- Helmsman turns the boat into the wind.
- Crew drops the mainsail and lifts and centreboard.
- Helmsman bears away, sailing under jib alone, and lifts the rudder blade a little as the water gets shallower.
- Crew jumps into the water and turns the boat head to wind.
- Helmsman drops the jib and removes the rudder. In strong winds with large waves it may not be possible for the crew to turn the boat head to wind with the jib up. The following method (which requires slightly more skill on behalf of the helmsman) may be used:
- Sail to the shore on a broad reach.
- Helmsman eases the mainsail and turns the boat into the wind.
- Crew jumps out of the boat and holds it head to wind.
- Helmsman drops the mainsail, removes the rudder and then drops the jib.

If you are blown aground on a lee shore unintentionally and cannot sail off again immediately, lower your sails. Do not raise the centreboard, because you will only be blown further on. To get afloat again, you can try rowing, paddling or hauling the boat off using the anchor.

Launching in an offshore wind

For novice crews an offshore wind can be very dangerous, as it is easy to sail away from the sheltered beach but more difficult to sail back. Offshore winds produce flat water close to the shore and the novice may be lured out into conditions which are beyond him. It is vital that an accurate estimate of wind strength is made before sailing with an offshore wind.

- Trolley the boat to the edge of the water and hoist the sails with the boat head to wind.
- If the onshore waves are not too big push the boat into the water and float it off the trolley still head to the wind. If the wind is not blowing directly off the shore, you might

Above: Launching; offshore wind. Below: Landing in an offshore wind.

prefer to launch before hoisting the sails.

- In larger waves, the boat may rise up with a wave then drop onto its trolley, damaging the hull. If there is any danger of this, carry the boat into the water (this may mean organising a team of helpers).

Leaving a beach, pontoon or jetty in an offshore wind is straightforward. The boat is held into the wind by the crew while the helmsman pulls a little rudder down.

- Crew pushes the bow of the boat away from the beach and the wind, and climbs into the windward side of the boat.
- With the main left slack, back the jib and the boat will head away from the shore. As soon as the water is deep enough pull the rudder right down and adjust the centreboard to suit the point of sailing.

Landing in an offshore wind

Landing is again relatively simple as long as one member of the crew accepts that he may get wet.

- Pick a suitable spot, with no underwater obstacles.
- Sail to a position where the landing site can be reached on a close hauled/close reach course, allowing for the extra leeway which will be made when the centreboard is raised.
- Sail towards the landing site and start to ease the sails to slow the boat down.
- Let fly the jib, and raise the centreboard and rudder according to depth.
- Ease the main. Crew jumps into the shallows and holds the shroud when the boat is at a standstill, then moves to the bow to hold the boat head to wind.
- Helmsman drops the sails, lifts the centreboard and removes the rudder.

Picking up and leaving a mooring in tidal water is a relatively simple process so long as the tidal stream is taken into account. You can assess the effect of the tide by looking at boats on swinging moorings, or looking at the flow of water past objects fixed to the sea bed.

Two methods can be used to pick up a mooring. One is used when wind and tide are in the same or similar directions. The second is used when wind and tide are opposed. With both methods it is vital that you assess your proposed route to or from the buoy. Estimate the direction of travel, taking into account the tidal stream and the amount of sail you are carrying.

Approaching a mooring – wind and tide together

- Check wind direction.
- Check tide direction.
- Choose a close-hauled or close-reach course to the buoy.
- Prepare the boat's mooring line.
- Let the jib fly.
- Ease the mainsail until the boat slows and eventually stops with the buoy on the windward side of the boat.
- Attach the mooring line.
- Drop sails.
- Lift centreboard and rudder.

Leaving a mooring – wind and tide together

- Check wind direction.
- Check tide direction and proposed route from buoy.
- Attach rudder.
- Hoist sails.
- Lower centreboard.
- Prepare mooring line for slipping.
- Pull the jib aback, slip the line and sail away close-hauled.

Approaching a mooring – wind and tide opposed

- Sail upwind of the mooring buoy, turn head to wind and drop the mainsail.
- Sailing under jib alone, head back against the tide to the mooring buoy (if the boat does not make way against the tide a little mainsail can be rehoisted).
- On reaching the mooring buoy let fly the jib.
- Secure a mooring line.

Leaving a mooring – wind and tide opposed

- Assess wind direction.
- Assess tide direction and proposed route.
- Hoist jib.
- Slip mooring line and sheet in the jib.
- Sail to an area with plenty of sea room and let the jib fly. Push the helm hard away and hoist mainsail.

Below: Approaching a mooring with wind and tide together.
Bottom: Leaving a mooring with wind and tide together.

Below: Approaching a mooring with wind and tide opposed.
Bottom: Leaving a mooring with wind and tide opposed.

Anchors are made to a variety of weights and patterns. An anchor is designed for the type of sea bed in which it is expected to be used, and for the size of the vessel it is to hold. The best dinghy anchor is undoubtedly a small CQR. Don't be tempted by the convenience of a folding grapnel anchor – they rarely work effectively.

THE CHAIN

A short length of chain attached to the anchor serves two purposes. It protects the warp from chafe on the seabed and its weight holds the shank of the anchor down, so helping it to bite into the seabed.

THE WARP

A warp (rope) of sufficient strength and length should be attached to the chain. The length will depend on the size of boat and the depth of water. You'll need a warp of at least three times (preferably five times) the greatest depth in which you want to anchor. To prevent chafe, the warp should always be fed through the bow fairlead. If your dinghy does not have a bow fairlead, you can improvise with a loop of line tied to the stemhead fitting.

STOWING THE ANCHOR AND WARP

The warp should be attached to the boat at a suitable strong point. On a sailing dinghy the base of the mast is usually a good place. Because the anchor may be needed quickly it must be stowed for instant use. It is also important that the warp should be able to run out freely. Stow it in loops coiled in a bucket, or on a drum.

Selecting an anchorage

When choosing a spot to anchor, consider the following points:

- Are there any underwater obstructions such as telephone cables?
- Will your anchor hold in the seabed?
- What is the depth of the water?
- How close are other water users, main channels etc? Will you swing into them?
- What is the expected tidal range?
- Will you drift on to a lee shore if the anchor drags?

Anchoring with wind and tide in similar directions

- Approach the chosen site on a close-hauled course.
- Prepare the anchor and lead it forward through the fairlead.

- Allow the boat to slow down by letting fly the jib and easing the main.
- When the boat has stopped, let go the anchor and allow the boat to drop back with wind and tide, paying out the anchor chain and warp.
- When enough has been paid out, check that the anchor is holding by reference to stationary objects – it's best to use two objects on the land which line up.
- Finally, lift the centreboard and drop the sails.

Below left and right: Anchoring with wind and tide together.
Bottom left: Securing the warp to the stemhead fitting.
Bottom right: A CQR anchor, chain and warp.

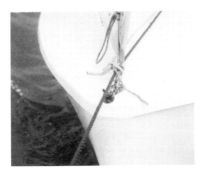

Anchoring with wind against tide

- Choose your site and sail upwind from it.
- Prepare the anchor, chain and warp.
- Sail head to wind and drop the mainsail.
- Sail downwind under jib alone. Ease the jib as you approach the chosen spot, then let the jib fly and lower the anchor.
- Again, check that the anchor is holding.
- Finally, lift the centreboard and lower the jib.

Below: Anchoring, wind against tide. (Top) Dropping the mainsail. (Bottom) Letting the jib fly.

Towing

A sailing dinghy which is being towed should have the sails lowered, the centreboard right up and the crew weight aft. Failure to do this will cause the dinghy to veer from one side to the other behind the towing vessel. Always lead the tow rope through the bow fairlead of the dinghy being towed and attach it to a suitable strong point.

PASSING A TOWLINE

In calm weather the two boats can simply lie alongside each other while the tow rope is passed across. In stronger winds the towing vessel should sail across the bows of the dinghy to be towed, on a close-hauled course from the leeward quarter, passing the towline as it goes. The sheets can be eased while the towline is made fast, before bearing away on a reach. In the case of a motor boat towing a sailing boat, if the motorboat is passing the line it should be thrown from upwind of the dinghy.

SECURING A TOWLINE

The strain of the towline must be spread over the whole boat and not transmitted to an individual fitting. In a sailing dinghy this usually means attaching it to the mast, or a thwart. Take a turn around the point where the towline is anchored. This will take the strain off the end of the rope, will prevent damage and injury, and will make it easier for you to secure the towline.

When the strain is taken up, there is a risk that the tow rope may break, or damage the dinghy being towed. The towing boat should always start slowly, and good communication between the two boats is vital. Work out a quick, simple set of signals.

Ropes are an essential part of every sailing boat's equipment. They are used to attach, raise and control the sails and to secure the boat to a jetty or mooring.

Over the centuries specific 'knots' have been developed for specific tasks. They may be called bends, hitches or knots but they all serve to attach one rope to another or to a solid object.

Securing ropes to cleats

When securing a rope to a cleat, first take a complete turn round the cleat before making two or three criss-cross turns over the 'horns'. If it is a warp or rope that is going to be in position for some time you can finish with a half-hitch. It is a convention to make the initial turn on a cleat right-handed – so that somebody else can release it easily.

Below: Securing a rope to a cleat.

Bowline

A most useful knot for forming a temporary eye, which will not slip if properly tied.

Round turn and two half hitches

An easy method of securing a line to the ring of a buoy, post or jetty.

Sheet bend

Used for joining two ropes together. Make the loop in the thicker rope first, then tie the knot as shown.

Figure of eight knot

A simple and very effective stopper knot, used to prevent the end of a rope running out through a block.

Clove hitch

Useful when securing a rope at intermediate points. If tied near the end of the rope, a half hitch on top gives added security.

Common whipping

Lay a loop of twine along the rope, then wind turns around tightly. Put the end through the loop, pull the protruding thread and cut off the loose ends.

Rolling hitch

A hitch with a variety of uses – securing to a post, through a ring, or to a long line.

Eyesplice

Tuck the strands under the standing part in the order shown. Each should be threaded through three times.

Heatsealing

The ends of most modern ropes can be heatsealed to prevent them fraying or unlaying, using a match or a gas flame. Professionals use a 'hot knife' to provide a cleaner finish.

The weather is a fundamental part of sailing, and those who sail tidal waters soon discover the effects of the tide. The dinghy sailor who takes to the water without considering these basic elements is certain to be caught out sooner or later. The consequences will inevitably be inconvenient; they could be tragic.

Weather

Some insight into what the weather is going to do is obviously an advantage, and any sailor who takes a boat to sea should certainly aquaint himself with the forecast for the region. It is unwise to rely too much on forecasts for large areas; dinghy sailors should seek more local information. Try the forecasts on local radio, telephone forecasts, or the local coastguard.

LOCAL CONDITIONS
Apart from the day-to-day variations monitored and predicted by the weather forecasters, there are a number of local weather effects which occur almost daily. On the coast, the most important of these are the land and sea breezes.

During the summer months much of the coastline experiences sea breezes. The land heats up faster than the sea in the morning, and the air above the land rises. Cooler air from the sea is drawn in to replace it. If there is already an onshore wind this wind strength is increased by the sea breeze; if there is an offshore wind the sea breeze may well cancel it out.

The sea breeze usually reaches its peak in mid-afternoon, dropping away in the evening to be replaced by the opposite effect, the land breeze. This is caused by the land cooling down faster than the sea: the air mass above the land cools,

descends and drains out to sea.

In addition to these two conditions there are also local wind effects caused by the geography of the area. One example is when the land breeze is funnelled out to sea through a river valley: boats sailing in the estuary experience a stronger offshore wind than those sailing further along the coast. Such effects can also be observed inland, especially when there are hills nearby which channel the air. Information on these local effects is usually available at the sailing club.

Tides

Even if you learn to sail on inland waters, it will probably not be long before you want to savour the extra dimension which sea sailing has to offer. In most parts of the world the tide makes an enormous difference to coastal sailing. It can affect *where* you go, *when* you can go, *how long* it will take and *how wet* the journey will be.

Tides are caused by water responding to the gravitational pull of the moon and, to a lesser extent, the sun. When sun, earth and moon are all in a line (at new moon and full moon) the combined effect of the sun and moon causes the particularly big tides which are called *spring tides*. In between these times, at the first and third quarters of the moon, the sun and moon are at right angles to each other and their smaller combined effect causes smaller *neap tides*. Spring tides are both higher and lower than neap tides.

The difference in height between successive high and low tides is known as the *range*. This difference produces a flow of water around the coast, called a *tidal stream*. When the tide is rising it is said to be *flooding* and when it is falling it is said to be *ebbing*.

TIDE TABLES
Information about what the tide is doing at any time can be found from tide tables, which give the predicted times of high and low water and the range of the tide for each day of the year. These predictions are based on information printed for 'Standard Ports'. Two corrections have to be made before these tables are used:
• Convert Greenwich Mean Time (GMT) to British Summer Time (BST) if applicable.
• Add on a correction for the secondary port that is nearest to the area to be sailed in.

When you are planning a day's sailing in tidal waters, first look at the tide tables to check that you will be sailing with the tide. It ought to be obvious that with a favourable 2-knot tide, a 4-knot dinghy will effectively be three times as fast as the same dinghy sailing against the tide, yet it is common to see boats struggling home against a foul tide as darkness falls. The right use of the tide will enhance any day's sailing; get it wrong and you could be in for a miserable time and a long journey home.

DIRECTION OF TIDAL STREAM
The direction of the tidal stream can be observed by:
• Boats at anchor or at a single mooring riding with the bow facing the stream.
• Buoys leaning away from the stream and water 'piling up' against the buoys.
• Water swirling round a post or uncovered object.
It is also useful to know that tidal streams flow faster in:
• Deep waters.
• Navigation channels.
• The third and fourth hours of ebb flood.
• Off headlands.
If such tidal streams are constricted or obstructed in any way

by headlands or an uneven sea bottom, then tidal rips, eddies and overfalls can occur causing turbulent seas, especially if the wind direction opposes that of the tidal stream. Rough water can also be expected over a harbour bar, due to the combination of wind, tide and restricted depth.

Below: The lie of the moored yacht and the flow past the post show the tide is flowing from right to left.

RULE OF TWELFTHS

The rule of twelfths is a rough guide to the proportion of the total range which the tide will rise or fall during any hour after high water (HW).
● During the first hour after HW the range will be 1/12th of the total.
● During the second hour after HW the range will be 2/12th of the total.
● During the third hour after HW the range will be 3/12th of the total.
● During the fourth hour after HW the range will be 3/12th of the total.
● During the fifth hour after HW the range will be 2/12th of the total.
● During the sixth hour after HW the range will be 1/12th of the total.
    The same rule can be used to calculate the hourly rate of the rising tide. The system is by no means accurate, but used with reference to the tide tables it will give an

indication of the depth of water at any time. It also indicates the rate of flow: obviously the further the tide falls or rises in any hour, the faster the tidal stream. Thus the flow is slowest near high or low water, and fastest in the third and fourth hours between the two.

Charts and pilotage

Charts are drawn using a system of latitude and longitude as a grid reference and a scale. Distance is always measured on the latitude scale (up the *side* of the chart) where one minute of latitude is equal to one nautical mile. The vertical lines on the chart all relate to true north.
    Charts may be out of date almost as soon as they are printed since the coastline, lights, buoys and other features are constantly changing. The date of the chart is printed on its bottom edge, and it may be up-dated from the relevant Admiralty Chart corrections (weekly or quarterly). Your chart dealer will advise on this.
    Charts vary in scale. For the dinghy sailor who is not going to travel very far, a large scale chart with a lot of detail is probably of most use.
    Virtually all modern charts measure depth in metres. Any chart that has soundings in fathoms is likely to be out of date. Depths are related to the Lowest Astronomical Tide (LAT) which is a theoretical lowest possible tide – much lower than a normal low tide. For example: $5_2 = 5.2$ metres of water at LAT.
    Soundings which are underlined are drying heights, and represent height *above* LAT. For example, a rock marked $\underline{6}$ dries six metres above LAT.
    The tide tables are also related to LAT, so the depth of water indicated

in the tide table, or worked out using the rule of twelfths, can be added to that shown on the chart.
    Buy a chart of your intended sailing water so that you can see the positions of channels, shallows, rocks and any other obstructions, and the buoys which mark them.

BUOYAGE

The important thing to remember when sailing a dinghy is that the buoyage system is principally for the masters of larger vessels. Dinghy sailors may actually find it safer to navigate outside the limits of navigable channels; you may still have enough depth in which to sail and you know you will be safe from shipping. Having said that, buoyage must be used in conjunction with a chart because it indicates the presence of shoals or other dangers.

TRANSITS

Although buoys from the principal aid to pilotage, the dinghy sailor may well find that, in particular circumstances, the use of transits will be valuable. A transit is formed when two identifiable objects are in line with each other. If those two objects are in line, then you know that you must be on a position line extending through the objects. This gives a very accurate position line without any reference to the compass or other navigational aid. In some cases the transits are deliberately established, such as the leading lights set up to provide a guide to a harbour entrance. In other cases the transits can be less formal. For example, you might see in local sailing directions that the transit formed by keeping one headland clear of another will keep you away from rocks or a shoal.
    When using transits it is wise to check the transit with a compass bearing to ensure that you have identified the objects correctly.

First aid is what it says it is. Immediate action, probably taken by an unskilled person. It is essential to get the patient proper, qualified medical aid as soon as possible.

Treatment of hypothermia

With water sports the worst danger is not drowning – as some people might think – but getting cold: hypothermia. Nobody enjoys being cold and wet for long, and discomfort can turn into danger if you do nothing about it. The simple message is: stay warm.

The symptoms of hypothermia depend on its severity. At first, a person may shiver, look cold and complain of cold. It is when the shivering and complaints stop that you know that he or she is getting worse and could die. Look out for drowsiness, confusion and lethargy, which may lead on to cramp, slurred speech, nausea and numbness in arms and legs and eventually unconsciousness.

When somebody clearly shows all these symptoms, never give alcohol. Re-warming with warm coverings and warm drinks is probably the best way to restore the 'body core' temperature. In severe cases, if somebody is not breathing, you may be able to help by giving mouth-to-mouth resuscitation (see

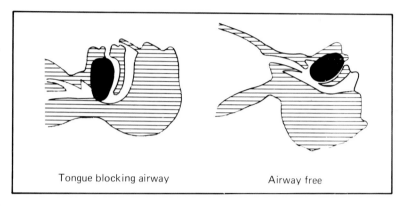

Tongue blocking airway   Airway free

below) and by getting qualified medical assistance to administer external cardiac compression (ECC).

Emergency resuscitation

If someone has stopped breathing, you must take over to ensure a supply of oxygen to the brain.
● First check whether the unconscious casualty has stopped breathing. Lay him on his back and look along his chest. If you can't hear, feel or see any signs of breathing, take action promptly.
● Place one hand under his neck, your other on his forehead and tilt his head back. This may be enough to clear the airway and start his breathing. If not, check the mouth and throat for obstructions and clear them.

● Take a deep breath, pinch the casualty's nostrils, seal your lips around his mouth and blow into his lungs until his chest rises.
● If it doesn't, check again for obstructions and clear them.
● Lift your head clear to watch the chest fall and give three more inflations in quick succession. This saturates his lungs with oxygen.
● Check the casualty's pulse. If the heart is beating, continue to give inflations at about 16 times a minute.
● If the heart has stopped, you must perform ECC. Learn how on a First Aid course.

NOTE
No AIDS infection is known to have occurred as a result of carrying out mouth to mouth resuscitation.